LEADERSHIP EXPERIENCES

Also by Timothy Johnson

Experiences: Lessons Learned as an Emerging Leader
Experiences: The Workbook for Emerging Leaders
Experiences: The Planner for Emerging Leaders

TIMOTHY JOHNSON

LEADERSHIP EXPERIENCES
The Series for Emerging Leaders

THIS BOOK IS A PRODUCT OF TRUTH PUBLICATIONS, LLC
TRUTHPUBLICATIONSLLC@GMAIL.COM

LEADERSHIP EXPERIENCES: THE SERIES FOR EMERGING LEADERS
ISBN: 978-1-7366112-0-3
COPYRIGHT © 2020 BY TIMOTHY JOHNSON

WRITTEN BY TIMOTHY JOHNSON
ALL RIGHTS RESERVED
NO REPRODUCTION OF THIS WORK, IN PART OR WHOLE, WITHOUT WRITTEN
CONSENT FROM THE AUTHOR IS PROHIBITED

Table of Contents

♦

Introduction i
Timeline ii
The Model iii

♦ ♦

Chapter 1: Define Your Purpose 1
Chapter 2: Where is the Power 9
Chapter 3: Establish Boundaries 17
Chapter 4: Level Up 25
Chapter 5: Align Your Mission 33
Chapter 6: Leadership is Not a Personality 39
Chapter 7: Be a River Not a Reservoir 49
Chapter 8: Surrounded by Greatness 59
Chapter 9: Still Serving 67
Chapter 10: The Planner 77

♦ ♦ ♦

References 115

Introduction

It is my hope that you have picked up this book because you are interested in assuming the role of leader, have just recently embarked on a leadership journey, or hold a tenured leadership role with inquisitiveness as to what tips an emerging leader has learned. It is also my hope that you find what you are looking for through practical strategies and principles in *Leadership Experiences*. In this series for emerging leaders, I will share with you the experiences that I have read and experienced, learned and experienced, or learned from experience. In 2009, I began a career in higher education as a full-time employee, and I would spend the next decade developing that career. In 2016, my leadership journey began as I had the opportunity to gain exposure to leadership development programs, literature, and experiences that would help shape me to fit the roles that I would begin to fill. I write this book not exclaiming my great leadership abilities. I write this book as a way to share my various experiences, provide an opportunity for reflection, and provide practical strategies to assist others in their leadership journey. I have had the great opportunity to participate in three, one-year leadership development training programs. Recognizing that not all individuals are afforded such opportunities, I felt compassion to share my experiences. The timeline below shares a short visual of my professional journey with regards to what will be shared in the ensuing chapters. I hope that this series will provide you with the practical tools to help ensure your success as you emerge as a leader in the specific endeavor you choose.

Timeline

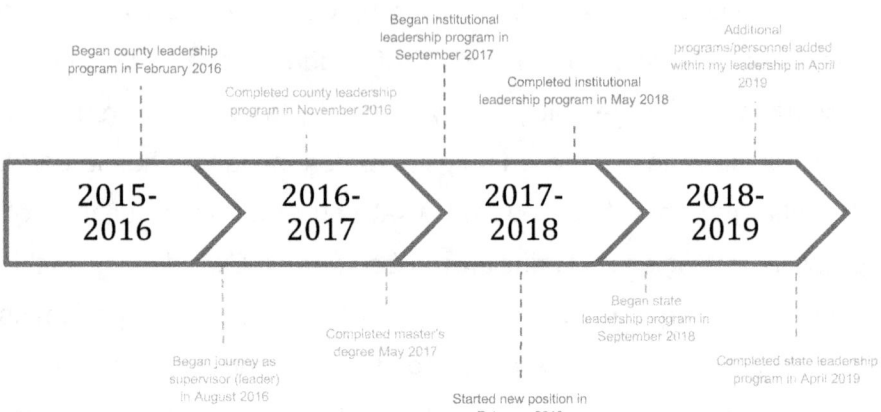

THE MODEL
for
EMERGING LEADERS

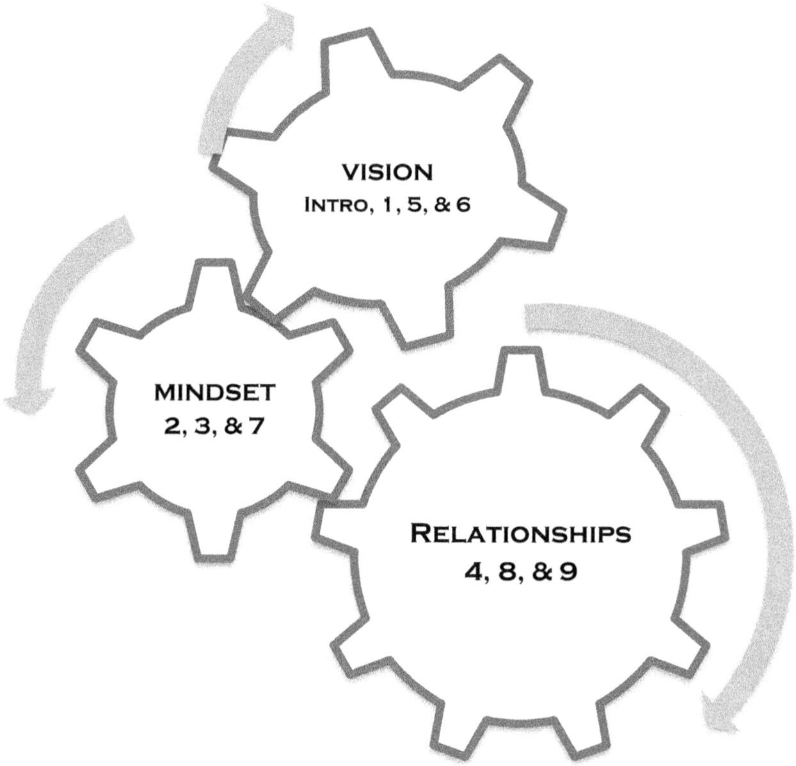

VISION
INTRO, 1, 5, & 6

MINDSET
2, 3, & 7

RELATIONSHIPS
4, 8, & 9

1

DEFINE YOUR PURPOSE

IT WAS A NORMAL DAY IN THE OFFICE. Seeing students and responding to emails were just a few items on the agenda. An email came from the president of the institution regarding a county leadership program that was sent to all faculty and staff of the college. The institution supports leadership development, so the administration would normally send an employee each year to this program. I immediately deleted the email. There was no interest on my part to participate in that particular program. However, interested candidates would complete the application and submit it to their supervisor. The institution also had its own internal leadership program that approximately six employees would engage in yearly. I remember thinking that while I was not currently interested in the internal leadership program, I would rather participate in it as opposed to the county program.

A few days after deleting the email, the vice president supervising the division in which I worked came into my office. Sitting down to have a conversation, I was curious as to what would follow. It was not unusual to have a conversation with the vice president. However, it would either be in his office or it would be a short, surface level conversation. Well, what would follow would be his reference to a meeting he had with the president where she stated she felt I would be a good candidate for the county leadership program. This came as a complete shock as I had put the leadership program out of my mind! Remember, I immediately deleted that email? The vice president followed up with his thoughts by saying that he agreed with her before referencing some of the accomplishments and tasks that I had completed. After the conversation, I agreed to submit an application for their review and recommendation.

At this point, it was a done deal. I had just agreed to participate and represent my institution in this county wide leadership program. Business and industry leaders, throughout the county, would each send one or two representatives from their companies to participate. Not only did I not feel like I was an emerging leader, I did not feel comfortable due to the debris of my previous environments.

While I grew up in a dual parent household, I grew up in a low-income environment. Often times, and in my case, this low socioeconomic status results in a lack of opportunities, exposure, and awareness. That being the said, I always had a desire to attend college. To prepare myself, I would take college preparatory courses in high school to put myself into a position to be ready if and when an opportunity presented itself. Taking these courses, however, often directed me away from classmates who looked like me or who may have been brought up in environments similar to mine. I often felt out of place and uncomfortable in those situations. So, when I say unaware and unexposed, I am referring back to those moments. I am referring to having a lack of opportunities. I am referring to the infrequent exposure to experiences outside of my hometown. I am referring to not having close friendships and relationships with peers. I am referring to not engaging in the traditional college experience enjoyed by those whom I sat in those college preparatory classes with (and their *peers* whom I would soon be gathering with to engage in leadership development).

While I would later become grateful for the opportunity to be selected for this program, the fact is, it was not my idea. I did not ask to attend. With that said, I did not have any identified goals or outcomes that I wanted to take away from the program. I would just go, try my best to represent my institution in a positive way, and "network." Most often with programs like this, networking and relationship building are high priority goals for participants. One of the top strategies related to networking or relationship building is finding common ground. Well, with me growing up with limited opportunities such as not taking family vacations or not having traditional experiences as an undergraduate, finding common ground came more difficult for me. However, for those who had similar experiences or interests (most everyone else), networking came more naturally. Additionally, I would learn that many individuals shared desires that I did not. I would soon realize that networking should not be my primary goal simply because others refer to it so often. Yes, it has its value; but I would instead need to define my own purpose for this program. Romans 12:2 tells us not to conform to the world. But instead, it tells us to be transformed by the renewing of our minds. I was conforming my goals and outcomes of the program to fit what the world - or others - thought should be my goal. Instead, I should make my goals fit for me. I should simply be grateful for the opportunity and commit to the work, time, and energy that would be needed to successfully complete this program. It was then when I realized I would enjoy the traveling experiences of going on industry tours. I would have an opportunity to now gain exposure and learn more about the county I grew up in but had little knowledge regarding. I would also learn more about personality types and actual tips and strategies that would help with leadership development.

For emerging leaders, this concept of defining your purpose is multi-faceted. It can echo what Steven Covey talks about with beginning with the end in mind[1]. It could help shape your core values. Maybe, it could help you develop a foundation to be persistent when challenging times occur - what Dr. Eric Thomas would define as your "Why"[2]. You may even take this concept of "Why" into account when looking at defining your purpose and understand the importance of not comparing yourself to others - something we will talk more about in chapter six. Finally, this concept directly correlates to vision or a plan. Without a vision, a goal, or a plan (intended outcomes), how will you be able to measure success? Define your purpose - intended outcomes - prior to engaging in a project, program, or task. Then, work toward that purpose.

SUMMARY

In chapter one of *Experiences: Lessons Learned as an Emerging Leader*, the concept of defining your purpose is explored. This is the notion of having intended outcomes or goals established prior to engaging in a project or task. The author shares his experience of not having defined goals prior to entering his first leadership development program. He also explains how he was able to put into prospective the typical goals that are usually associated with such programs while defining his own goals based on his past experiences and future interest.

> "Well, with me growing up with limited opportunities such as not taking family vacations or not having traditional experiences as an undergraduate, finding common ground came more difficult for me."

THEORY

- Steven Covey 7 Habits of Highly Effective People: Habit One - Begin with the end in mind.
- Dr. Eric Thomas: What's your Why?
- Without a vision, a goal, or a plan (intended outcomes), how will you be able to measure success?

DEFINE YOUR PURPOSE

REFLECTION

What activities (projects, programs, or tasks) have you begun within the past 12 months that you did not have any intended outcomes for? Did you have outcomes but they did not fit you personally?

Activity	Did you have intended outcomes	If so, did they fit your purpose	What could have been better outcomes
	Yes / No	Yes / No	
	Yes / No	Yes / No	
	Yes / No	Yes / No	
	Yes / No	Yes / No	

APPLICATION

What upcoming activities (projects, programs, or tasks) do you have that you should develop intended outcomes for? Develop them here.

Upcoming Activity	Intended Outcome	Rationale (Your "Why")

2

WHERE IS THE POWER

AS TIME TRANSPIRED, it was revealed to me one of the reasons the president thought I would be a good candidate for the leadership program. We were on the verge of securing funds that would significantly impact my position. At the time, I was traveling to the area high schools to help juniors and seniors with college readiness activities. The new funds would allow a more comprehensive approach to this process by placing college personnel into the five school districts to work with students from grades 7-12. I later learned that I would play a significant role as I would be tasked with assembling this team of four. I would be responsible for leading the process of hiring, training, planning, organizing, leading, and controlling.

While I would be directly over the management of the grant and staff, the president had a large role in securing the funds. She led a committee through research done at the state level to identify best practices within college readiness. The vice president had a great deal of involvement as well, being he was the author of the grant proposal. Needless to say, many people were vested into this program, and I had eyes on me and this project.

Thinking back to the initial interviews with the new staff, a decision needed to be made as it related to which school districts each of the individuals would be placed. While others had their opinions, I knew where "I" wanted to place them individually within the five districts. During the initial week of training, I remember talking with the new staff regarding reporting. I thought about how I wanted information, and "I" asked them to provide reports based off that desire. I recall thinking about how I wanted to facilitate team building; so, "I" set a schedule for team meetings. I even remember when the president wanted routine updates. My approach stayed the same as I articulated to the staff, "I would like for you to do...". This is the concept of not giving your power (or authority) away[3].

Had I begun every request I had (or the administration had) with "the president wants..." or "the vice president wants...", I would have been diminishing my authority and power as their leader. I would have been transferring it directly to the president and vice president. Instead, these individuals (the administration) empowered and entrusted "me" with this program and the responsibility; so, "I" would not give "them" back the power they just gave to me. For if I did begin every request to my team with "the president" or "the vice president," they would have never saw me as their leader, and I would have never had the opportunity to grow as their leader. It would have weakened the chain of command; and when "I" actually needed or wanted something from them, there could be less urgency on their part to provide that information for me. When I did have a vision for the program, there could be more, or less, buy-in depending on who they perceived the vision came from. As the leader, you are spending time with the employees that are within your oversight. You are developing a relationship with them. If you want to "Level Up" as a leader (a concept we will learn in chapter 4), do not give your power away. Develop a relationship with your team by sharing your vision, goals, and desires. And, as you articulate a call to action, as you articulate or inspire a shared vision, your request and/or vision will be better received."

SUMMARY

Chapter two shares an illustration of ownership by encouraging emerging leaders not to give away their power. An easy way for emerging leaders to lose influence with their team – or struggle to gain influence – is to constantly frame their comments or desires as request from a higher level of leadership. Despite having higher-level leaders take interest in a project the author was working on, he was able to show simple examples of how he did not give his power away. This concept encourages emerging leaders to take ownership when communicating with their team – even if the request does come from a higher level. This shows your team that you have leadership competencies which can help develop your influence with them.

> "For if I did begin every request to my team with "the president" or "the vice president," they would have never saw me as their leader, and I would have never had the opportunity to grow as their leader."

THEORY

A **Microwave Mentality** is an attitude or thought process suggesting that results should occur instantly. This mentality is usually unsuccessful as it can potentially provide results for the immediate future, but the process does not provide an adequate foundation for results to be sustained or ongoing. While trusting the process and **sowing seeds** may take a while longer to witness results, if sown on good ground, results will be forthcoming, sustainable, and ongoing.

In the example of framing comments from a higher level of leadership, results may come more rapidly if request were framed from that perspective. However, one would be losing valuable opportunities to sow seeds of growth as a leader. Is sacrificing the long-term for the immediate worth the potential long-term implications?

REFLECTION

I typically *sow seeds* for sustainable results even if they take longer to see rather than looking for immediate results.

1 – Never	2 – Rarely	3 – Sometimes	4 – Often	5 – Always

I find it more difficult to achieve results taking the long route and going through a process.

1 – Disagree	2 – Somewhat Disagree	3 – Neutral	4 – Somewhat Agree	5 – Agree

I believe that, with practice, I will be able to achieve success not always looking for immediate results.

1 – Disagree	2 – Somewhat Disagree	3 – Neutral	4 – Somewhat Agree	5 – Agree

APPLICATION

Develop a relationship with your team by sharing your vision, goals, and desires. And, as you articulate a call to action, as you articulate or inspire a shared vision, your request and/or vision will be better received.

What is the vision for the area that you lead? _____

_____

_____

How will this vision impact your team? _____

_____

_____

How will you articulate your vision? _____

_____

_____

How will you gain buy-in for your vision? _____

_____

_____

WHERE IS THE POWER

What strategies will help you to stay the course if results (or buy-in) are not immediate? _____

_____
_____
_____
_____
_____
_____
_____
_____

LEADERSHIP EXPERIENCES

Write additional takeaways here.

3

Establish Boundaries

AS I CONTINUED TO GROW into this role of leader, I was mindful of looking for intended outcomes in various situations. I knew putting four individuals, who were at different points in their careers with very different talents and personalities, together would require providing environments to help them grow as a team. Creating and providing this environment would be necessary for efficiency in sharing best practices, cultivating positive energy, and promoting unity when others needed assistance. I knew after this team was formed that I would need to be strategic in creating an environment to provide opportunities for these individuals to go through the process of team building.

One of the first things I asked the new employees to do during their first week of training was to exchange phone numbers. While this could have taken place organically, I found it important that I go ahead and facilitate this process to ensure proper, inclusive communication. I would also initiate a group message to normalize their early communication with each other. Eventually, I would remove myself from such communications to allow horizontal communication between the team.

An opportunity presented itself in the form of a yearlong professional development opportunity. This opportunity would put the staff into a position to learn content related to their job that would culminate in positioning them to receive a credential pertinent to their position. It was also pertinent to my position, and I had been interested in going through this training for some time. However, a conflict would always arise preventing me from participating. I notified the team of this opportunity and encouraged them to apply. I would do the same. This meant five applications from our institution had been submitted. I was later notified - as the supervisor - that only three of the five applicants could be accepted due to space. It was up to me to select the three. I chose to remove myself, and I used wisdom on choosing between the others. It was an easy decision to remove myself knowing how important it is to provide opportunities for the employees to grow. With me choosing myself over an employee, I would not be modeling this principle. I also wanted the group to begin to bond without me. Since this opportunity would require monthly webinars and four overnight trips, this was a good opportunity to help facilitate that bonding.

Because the employees would be giving presentations to students routinely, I wanted to assess their knowledge of various topics, assess their presentation skills, and provide an opportunity for them to teach/reinforce the information with each other. During their first week in "the field", they were given a few assignments including developing a presentation on identified topics. These presentations were to be presented by them to the team and myself at the end of the week. This proved to be a valuable exercise. Each individual developed their presentations and delivered them. One employee in particular struggled. I did not throw a lifeline. Imagine a new employee, surrounded by the boss and fellow colleagues, struggling to deliver this presentation. To see how each team member showed support, encouragement, and guidance was great. It was not my intention to embarrass this employee. It was my intention to monitor the responses from her and the group and help them grow through this experience.

Other methods were employed to create environments to facilitate team building and progression through group dynamics. We established team meetings once every three weeks to share successes, struggles, best practices, in-house professional development, and updates. We held a small potluck during the holiday season; and when one of the employees moved out of state, we held one then. I even had the staff privately write down key attributes about the other team members that I would incorporate into the next team meeting. After explaining some information at one of the team meetings, I would leave the room so the group could talk amongst themselves and reflect without my presence.

During these processes, one key concept stood out to me. I noticed how important it was for me to step back from the team. It was important for me to help facilitate communication and a positive environment in the earlier parts of this process, but it was even more important to know when to begin stepping back. I could not continue going to lunch with the team every time they went together. The conversations I would have with the team would become more limited than those they would have with each other. In stepping back, I had to create appropriate boundaries as the leader. I needed to observe how they began and continued to interact with each other. I could still enjoy and ensure a good environment. However, I needed to also ensure that when I needed to hold any one of the employees accountable, set an expectation, or conduct an evaluation, I would be able to do so with a good conscience and without self-created barriers that I would have created from not establishing appropriate boundaries. It would ensure that a respect factor existed; and if it did not exist, it would not be from something that I facilitated or endorsed as their leader. Establish boundaries to ensure respect, but do not be distant from those who look to you for support. Do not miss the opportunity to develop a relationship, mentor, or even learn from (and about) your employees. Do not misinterpret this principle as non-relational. An effective leader has to be relational. However, understand that in certain areas, there must be appropriate boundaries.

SUMMARY

Establishing Boundaries is the focal point of chapter three. The author gave various examples of facilitating an appropriate environment but shared the importance of stepping back after ensuring the environment is developed. Phrases such as "to ensure proper, inclusive communication" and "normalize their early communication with each other" were mentioned in this chapter.

> "It was important for me to help facilitate communication and a positive environment in the earlier parts of this process, but it was even more important to know when to begin stepping back."

The author also talked about providing your staff with opportunities to grow and develop.

THEORY

Developmental Ecology and the components of Urie Bronfenbrenner's Theory highlight four main components – Process, Person, Context, and Time (or PPCT). Looking at the interaction between PPCT, it demonstrates how development is either promoted or inhibited. In the Context component, the Person is in the center (or focus) with four Context levels on the peripheral. The first two levels include the **microsystem and mesosystem**. The microsystem is, in summary, the relationship between the Person and their immediate environment while the mesosystem is the connection that takes place between multiple microsystems.

It was important for the author – as the leader – to begin stepping back to facilitate the development of his mesosystem. Consider the author as the focus – in the center. In this example, the individual employees (4) made up four separate microsystems for the leader. The individual employees' interaction/relationship with each other was the leader's mesosystem. How the individual employees interacted with each other would have an impact on the success of the program and his development as a leader.

There is another theory to be mindful of in the development of a team (or in this context – a mesosystem). This theory is **Tuckman's**

Stages of Group Development. It includes the following stages: Forming, Storming, Norming, Performing, and Adjourning. Forming is the assembling of a new team. Storming is when the new team begin to experience controversy in the process of figuring things out. The next stage, Norming, is when individuals in the team learns their role within the team. It is then that the team can begin working effectively toward that goal – which is performing. Finally, adjourning is when the team is complete with the task and part ways. Tuckman suggests that for a group to be an effective, high performing team, it must successfully progress through these stages.

REFLECTION

Use these questions as discussion prompts with a group of leaders/emerging leaders.

1. What strategies have you used when first assembling a team?
2. What follow up strategies have you used to facilitate team building?
3. What strategies have you employed to facilitate accountability?
4. What strategies have you conducted to ensure continuous improvement?

    Write your individual notes here _____
    _____
    _____
    _____
    _____
    _____
    _____

APPLICATION

List takeaways that you learned from the group discussion through the reflection process and place them in one of the categories below. Proceed accordingly.

Will take Longer to Implement	Can Implement but need more work	Can Implement Right Away

Write additional notes, reflections, or actionable items here.

4

LEVEL UP

REFLECTING ON THE MAKEUP of the team members, those selected included a co-worker, a new professional, and two individuals new to higher education. Of the four, I was familiar with the co-worker, but had no previous relationships with any of the others. The co-worker knew a little about my journey at the institution. The other three - to my knowledge - knew nothing about me. In their new positions, they were all going to follow me only because of my position as their supervisor.

Halfway through the academic year, one of the original team members was replaced due to relocation. Throughout the hiring process to replace this individual, my first interaction with the new team member would be during this time. Again, this would mean she would only follow me because of my position as supervisor. As these positions were essentially entry-level positions, two more positions would be replaced before I transitioned to a higher role within the institution.

At some point prior to having the position of leader, I read some of the work by John C. Maxwell. One concept that Maxwell writes about is the five levels of leadership. Maxwell suggests that people will follow you as a leader first because they have to due to your position. Then, they may continue to follow you because they actually want to, because you have built a relationship with them. This is by permission. Next, individuals will want to follow you based on the results that you have achieved for your institution or organization. This level is called production. When you have success in helping people, this is another level of leadership. People want to follow you because of what you do for them. This is called people development. Finally, the fifth level is the pinnacle. It means people follow you because of your values, what you represent, and who you are[4].

These levels can be visualized as a pyramid or a staircase. You progress from the first level through the top level. The thing that was intriguing about these leadership levels is that not all employees have to be on the same level at the same time. This was interesting to me because as I worked to support the team as they worked directly with students, I worked as their supervisor. I was genuine. I served alongside them at evening workshops. I gave them freedom to put their talents on particular projects so long as it flowed through the overall vision. I supported their professional journeys and professional development. I hosted (on behalf of the institution) a statewide workshop where the team would see me work tirelessly to represent the institution well. They saw me serve as chair on one of the institution's committees. They saw how prepared I came to the team meetings highlighting their success. They recognized how I provided feedback and an environment for each other to share safely. They enjoyed me giving them an opportunity to share with administration the great work they had done on the secondary campuses rather than me giving the full update. They witnessed many positive characteristics that I embodied that would help them move up the staircase of my leadership. Yet, I was reminded that everyone would not be on the same level! I noticed through all that I did as a servant leader - who believe in developing people - that I had not progressed from leading by position with the full team.

Be mindful of the factors that lead to greater influence among those whom you lead, but be genuine in your leadership and approach to leadership. Level up! With that said, be mindful - and do not be discouraged - when your staff does not progress at the same pace, or at all, up the figurative leadership staircase.

SUMMARY

The author uses John C. Maxwell's concept of the Five Levels of Leadership in this chapter to explain the concept of leveling up. While great strides were made, organically, that should have boosted his influence or level of leadership with his staff, not all staff advanced to the same level nor at the same time. This chapter was a reminder that no matter how hard you work, lead, and prepare, some people – be it staff, co-workers, or other – will still struggle to see you as anything more than they initially saw

> "They witnessed many positive characteristics that I embodied that would help them move up the staircase of my leadership. Yet, I was reminded that everyone would not be on the same level!"

you as. You should not work to correct this. You should continue to prepare, lead, and be concerned with what is in your power to change.

THEORY

John C. Maxwell's literature serves as the backdrop for this chapter. Maxwell also has literature related to the various laws of leadership. One of the author's favorite laws from this literature is **the Law of the Process**. This law, while can be interpreted and applied in different ways, closely resembles what was shared in Chapter 3 related to short-term and long-term progress. Maxwell uses the analogy of the stock market and compound interest to establish the importance of personal growth and leadership development. He emphasizes a personal plan of growth and the investment into others. In order to effectively and organically grow your level of leadership, being process oriented is essential. It is daily development.

This chapter also helps set the stage to discuss **character vs. reputation**. When it is said to organically "Level Up", one must trust the process and do the right thing even when no one is watching. That is character. Tony Dungy states that "Character is tested, revealed, and further developed by the decisions we make in the most challenging times." Being a leader will not be easy. There will surely be challenging times that will occur. Remember, however, the quote from Dungy that this is when character is tested and revealed in these decisions. Dungy also establishes the connection of integrity to character stating it "is critical to everything we do because it is the foundation of trustworthiness in our own eyes…" Finally, the comparison of integrity to reputation is explored as he states, "our reputation is the public perception of our integrity." We hope to "Level Up", but it is up to the employees to witness the leader's value for themselves. Sadly, they will remain stagnant at times potentially due to reputation – a public perception of integrity. For others, reputation may not be the barrier, it may be time. In this case, **the Law of the Process** will work in your favor if you do the right things day in and day out while developing as a leader.

REFLECTION

- It is easy to display character in tough situations: True | False
- Displaying character over time is an easy task: True | False
- My reputation is more important than my character: True | False
- Although displaying character in certain situations is tough, I will commit to it: True | False
- Although displaying character over time is challenging, I will commit to the process: True | False
- I will exercise and develop my character for myself personally and whatever results follow will be added bonuses: True | False

APPLICATION

Looking at the next seven days, what tough decisions do you know you will need to respond to? What tough situations do you anticipate forthcoming? What conversations will you have to change your response to in order to better develop your character? What environments do you need to avoid that would stunt your character development?

Decisions:
_____
_____
_____

Situations:
_____
_____
_____

Conversations:
_____
_____
_____

Environments:
_____
_____
_____

Other:
_____
_____
_____

5

ALIGN YOUR MISSION

IN THE SUMMER OF 2016, I took a graduate course focused on budgeting and finance in higher education. The course emphasized the importance of mission which led us to review mission statements for institutions and organizations as well as strategic plans. Then, we would look at the correlating budgets to see if the budget aligned with what was said to be a priority (or the focus) of that institution/organization. This practice/concept was enlightening to me during this course.

In August of that same year, the program began that would designate me a leader by position, and I would complete the county leadership program in November of that year. I like to think between November 2016 and July 2017, I progressed from a positional leader to a level of permission and production with most of the team. I finished my graduate degree. I lead three summer programs and served as partner for another program. I provided national, professional development opportunities for each team member. I chaired a committee which helped provide needed structure. I led this new staff who helped increase the college going rate for the county that year by 6.7 percent. I would be recognized in front of the institution - by the institution - as the professional staff member of the year. A lot transpired during that academic year! One thing that transpired between January and May, specifically, was the institution president personally asking me when I would apply for the internal leadership program. Remember, I did think to myself that I would rather go through the internal leadership program before the county program. Well, I had completed the county program in November, and I would be done with my graduate program by the start of the internal program. I had a year of experience overseeing the new program. I had no ~~excuses~~ reasons not to apply. Side note: Isn't it interesting that we look for excuses not to do something that could add value to ourselves? In this case, it is the leadership program. However, it could be as simple as reading a book, watching a Ted Talk, having a Q&A session with a mentor or someone you think highly towards. The quote "It is not the things we do in life that we regret..., it is the things that we do not" from Randy Pausch[5] is one that I now use often.

    Needless to say, I applied for the internal program, was accepted, and would begin in September 2017 - along with five other colleagues. I defined my purpose (intended outcomes) for this program before beginning. During one of our sessions, a member from our administration led us through a hands-on task in which we had to decide as a group how to accomplish it. The task would require us to critically think; but more importantly, it made us look at the concept of making tough decisions. After the task was completed, she provided feedback as she had observed what went into our decisions and how we made those decisions. As we went through this task, I was reminded of the budgeting and finance course that talked about mission being the focus of what an individual or group does and prioritizing resources to align with it. That was what this task was about. It was about mission. It was asking, "What would we be willing to contribute and/or sacrifice to accomplish the mission?".

Another component of this program included the development of an individual portfolio which would include a personal mission statement. Institutions, organizations, and companies all have mission statements. Why not develop a personal mission statement to guide or ground your personal life? This concept could help to identify personal core values, and it gives individuals a reflection point when making decisions. Develop a personal mission statement, and align your thoughts, actions, words, and resources with your mission. Your mission should help you make decisions based on core values and principles rather than the emotion of the time.

SUMMARY

In this chapter, the author shares examples from a few of his experiences that emphasized the concept of mission. He also took a detour midchapter to share an example and quote regarding taking advantages of opportunities compared to making excuses and choosing not to take the opportunity. The quote used was from Randy Pausch which stated, "It is not the things we do in life that we regret..., it is the things that we do not." The author finished the chapter by talking about the importance of developing a personal mission statement. This statement can help you make decisions based on your values and principles rather than the emotion of the time.

> "Your mission should help you make decisions based on core values and principles rather than the emotion of the time."

THEORY

- Steven Covey: *7 Habits of Highly Effective People*
  https://msb.franklincovey.com/inspired/mission_statement_examples
- "Anyone can steer the ship, but it takes a leader to chart the course." John C. Maxwell: The Law of Navigation

REFLECTION

What is the mission of the company you currently work for?
_____
_____

What key words do you find in this mission?
_____

APPLICATION

Go to one (or both) of the sites below and follow the prompts.

https://msb.franklincovey.com/missions/freewrite/1

and/or

https://msb.franklincovey.com/missions/personal/1

Copy your results here.

6

LEADERSHIP IS NOT A PERSONALITY

DURING THE INTERNAL LEADERSHIP PROGRAM, we took a personality assessment and learned about our results. Afterwards, we would think about the specific characteristics of the assessments and try to identify which administrator had which results on the assessment. Each administrator had a different personality type.

As my colleagues (those in the internal leadership program) and I progressed through this program, different administrators would lead given sessions. One administrator chose to dialog back and forth with us sharing various examples along her career path. Another administrator used a few stories to metaphorically describe leadership as he led the session in a lecture format. Using quotes and questions, one administrator allowed my colleagues and me to drive the session. Hands-on learning was the preference of another administrator, while the last administrator brought his staff in to lead various sections of that session. Each administrator had a different style in their approach to leading their session. Could this be based on their preference for a particular personality type? Could this be based on other characteristics outside of a preference for a particular personality type?

After the internal program, I was recommended by our administration to attend a statewide leadership program and was selected. During the first session of this program, we were given a personality assessment - different from the assessment from the internal program. With the statewide program, there were individuals in leadership (and individuals aspiring to be in leadership) from institutions throughout the state. Yet, not all of the members were grouped into the same personality type. How was this possible?

At another session as a member of the statewide program, we had the privilege of learning from the administration from another community college. Before us sat the president, three vice presidents, and other administrators. I was familiar with some of the president's initiatives from communicating with the staff previously. I had also visited the website and learned of various initiatives, so I knew he was a visionary and would allocate resources accordingly [remember chapter 5]. As we learned from this group's Q&A, I could not help but notice how often the president allowed the other administrators to answer questions, share their experiences, and share their knowledge with us. Could this be based on a personality preference? Could this be based on a particular leadership style or leadership theory?

I give these examples of personalities because often times when we think of leaders, we may tend to think of an outgoing individual with excellent oration skills. While leaders should possess a certain measure of various competencies, leadership is not a personality. A leader does not have to have a preference for extroversion. A leader may have a preference for introversion but knows how to listen, think before speaking, and provide others opportunities to be heard. For leaders who refuse to listen will eventually be surrounded by people who have nothing significant to say.[6] A leader may or may not make most of their decisions based on intuition. A leader may have a different preference. Just because an individual is outspoken does not mean they are a leader. Just because an individual is quiet does not mean they are not a leader. I have heard the saying "lead by example" which means one should model the way to leadership and while in leadership, do not conform to thinking that you have to be heard or you have to say something at a given time because you are the leader. Allow your words to flow genuinely and organically. If you like to rationalize before making decisions, rationalize. If you like to use instinct and make quick decisions, go for it. Do not change what got you to this point. Yes, continue to develop your skills. Continue to be a lifelong learner. Continue to be humble, but do not alter what put you into this position as an emerging leader because you feel you need to "have a certain personality" now that you are a leader. You are a leader for the way you conducted business prior to becoming a leader. The way you chaired a committee when you were not in the position of leader. The way you showed up to work on time each day. The way you listened to your colleagues when they needed someone to talk to. The way you changed the tone of the conversation when co-workers complained to you about situations. These are the reasons you may have been given this opportunity. People see you as a leader before you ever assume the role of leader. These examples, and this concept, is also beneficial as we think of the potential of leading your current co-workers. Had I always complained, talked about others, and displayed poor work ethic around my co-workers, do you think my co-worker, who I would later lead, would have had respect for me even on the positional level mentioned in chapter 4? If you continue on this leadership journey, you will lead some of your current co-workers or those in your professional network that share similar positions to you now. No matter your personality preference, you can acquire and develop leadership competencies desired for a specific role and achieve that status. You will also learn how to flex your personality preference when necessary and appropriate. Do not be discouraged because your personality preferences do not align with those leaders that you may know. Personality preferences are important. They are important to know. They are important recognize. They are important to establish knowledge and appreciation of differences. Ultimately, being able to effectively identify and utilize these differences can lead to synergy. Knowing these preferences can lead to better teamwork, decision making, and problem solving. However, leadership is not a particular personality. In fact, Michael Segovia suggests that "True leadership is the ability to flex to what those who follow you need." [7]

SUMMARY

As a certified practitioner for the MBTI® assessment, the author uses his training to share the concept of appreciating differences. Before becoming certified, however, the author took some form of personality assessment during each leadership program. Noticing how diverse the results were among aspiring leaders, it was evident that leadership was not a personality. It is extremely beneficial to know and recognize your personality type. This will allow you more clarity as to how you take in information and make decisions. However, since leaders share various personality preferences (and the individuals they will be leading will likely have different preferences), it allows you the ability to know your *blind spots* as a leader and intentionally *flex* when appropriate. The author also touches on the fact that leadership competencies do exist, but also that they can be learned.

> "While leaders should possess a certain measure of various competencies, leadership is not a personality."

THEORY

It is a fundamental concept that in order to successfully lead an organization, you must be able to effectively lead others; and in order to effectively lead others, you must effectively **lead yourself** first. Leading yourself deals greatly with self-awareness. Learning your biases and what stimulates your drive are just two examples of self-awareness. Being able to manage these examples (and many other examples of self-awareness) are what helps you to effectively

LEADERSHIP IS NOT A PERSONALITY

lead self. While leadership is not a personality, personality is a starting point to understanding self. Various self-assessments help individuals to better appreciate differences, understand decision making, and provide information to help individuals develop in needed areas.

REFLECTION

What is your level of awareness in some key areas of leading yourself? Using the prompts on the next page, use the "S" in the "S/N" option to indicate if you feel you are strong in this area or use the "N" to indicate if you feel you need improvement in this area. Next, shade in the shape(s) in the *Level of Awareness* box to indicate how sure you are of your decision. Zero shades would indicate that you are unsure while 10 shades would indicate that you are very sure.

LEADERSHIP EXPERIENCES

AREAS OF REFLECTION	LEVEL OF AWARENESS
Discipline (S/N)	◊ ◊ ◊ ◊ ◊ ◊ ◊ ◊ ◊
Consistency (S/N)	◊ ◊ ◊ ◊ ◊ ◊ ◊ ◊ ◊
Character (S/N)	◊ ◊ ◊ ◊ ◊ ◊ ◊ ◊ ◊
Avoiding Bias (S/N)	◊ ◊ ◊ ◊ ◊ ◊ ◊ ◊ ◊
Relationships (S/N)	◊ ◊ ◊ ◊ ◊ ◊ ◊ ◊ ◊
Individuality (S/N)	◊ ◊ ◊ ◊ ◊ ◊ ◊ ◊ ◊
Lifelong Learner (S/N)	◊ ◊ ◊ ◊ ◊ ◊ ◊ ◊ ◊
Honesty (S/N)	◊ ◊ ◊ ◊ ◊ ◊ ◊ ◊ ◊
Focus (S/N)	◊ ◊ ◊ ◊ ◊ ◊ ◊ ◊ ◊

E/A

APPLICATION

Look at the areas with five shades or less. Write these areas here.

_____

Write the areas that you selected "N" which indicated that you felt you needed improvement here. _____

_____

Use this information to find various resources such as books, videos, and/or websites or conduct informational interviews with others to help you to understand your uncertainty, develop in your awareness of an area, and expand your capacity to develop in the area. Be intentional in your development in order to better lead yourself, lead others, and lead organization.

If you are interested in taking the MBTI® assessment, contact the author at truthpublicationsllc@gmail.com. The Myer-Briggs® Company offers the MBTI® Complete which is an online, interactive learning process that allows you take the full MBTI assessment on your own timetable and at your own pace. You will learn type and how it works. You will also be able to determine your four-letter type. You will learn how your type interacts with others, your type strengths, and important areas of growth.

Best Fit Type

7

BE A RIVER NOT A RESERVOIR

MERRIAM WEBSTER EXPLAINS THAT a river is a natural stream of water of usually considerable volume. Looking into that definition at the word stream, one may visualize a stream as a body of running water. Another way to define stream is a constantly renewed or steady supply. Whereas a reservoir is a place where something is kept in store. A reservoir is a reserve[8]. It is good to have a specific amount of reserve, but a reserve has the ability to run out. A river is a constant supply. Thinking of natural resources and elements, Oxygen - like water - is something that can be found in a steady supply or kept in store. An example is on an aircraft. Conditioned air, in a specific amount, is pumped into the cabin of an aircraft so that those aboard the aircraft are comfortable and safe at such high altitudes. Have you ever been on a plane and heard something similar to this phase?

> *"Oxygen and the air pressure are always being monitored. In the event of a decompression, an oxygen mask will appear in front of you. To start the flow of oxygen, pull the mask towards you. Place the mask firmly over your nose and mouth, secure the elastic band behind your head, and breathe normally. If you are travelling with a child or someone who requires assistance, secure your mask on first, and then assist the other person."*[9]

In the aircraft example, failure to secure your mask first could quickly result in your body not receiving enough oxygen which would leave you passed out and not being of use to the person or persons that were depending on you. These two examples are directly correlated to self-care.

Self-care is the intentional practice of reducing stress and increasing well-being. Well-being is present in the physical, mental, emotional, and spiritual forms. There are various ways that we can intentionally engage in self-care. One of these is to focus on productivity. We have our careers and are expected to produce. Sometimes we may have multiple responsibilities and may find ourselves very busy. With productivity and self-care, however, we should make sure that we are not too busy being busy that we are not being productive. Instead, we should focus on time management and - when necessary - look to simplify things when we get too lost in the details. This concept of production includes meeting metrics. It includes implementing strategies as a result of vision. It includes executing tasks, but it also includes taking care of yourself. More practical ways to take care of yourself is by utilizing the benefits that your employer included into your compensation package. One of the quickest and easiest ways to build resentment toward you career or company/institution is to neglect self for company. When you begin to work weekends as the norm, work from home as the norm, and fail to make routine doctor visits because you do not have time, this can lead to the other end of self-care which is burnout. I remember talking with my pastor one night. I recall saying that I earn vacation time, but I usually do not take it because I am so busy in my position. As I spoke those words, I remember hearing how delusional it sounded even as it came from my mouth. We may be great at what we do. We may have endless projects that we think have endings, but we must remember the concept of the oxygen mask. We must take care of ourselves first so that we can then take care of or benefit others.

After reading and listening to various materials, I highly recommend developing a routine to serve as an ongoing, continuous way to facilitate self-care. There was an exercise I saw that gave the reader instructions to write down 10 things - that when done - you are at your happiest or best. Then you would circle three and commit to doing those three things every day. I focused on a morning routine consisting of various elements - and continue to modify it. I noticed when I wake up early, my mornings tend to run much smoother. I am not in such a hurry, and once I do the other three or so things identified that make me happy, within 4 ½ hours (8:30 AM), I am typically in a good space mentally, physically, emotionally, and spiritually. When parts of my routine are off (such as not agreeing with the early morning alarm), I may find myself working harder to get into a better frame of mind approaching the other parts of my day. However, my day is not completely off. I may not have as much positive momentum as I could have had; but self-care, too, is recognizing that one moment, situation, or experience does not dictate the direction of your day. It has the power to build positive or negative momentum; but we have the power to produce constant, positive thoughts and momentum from those positive thoughts. A routine of things, that when you do them, you are at your best is something I encourage you to look to implement now and adjust as needed. For me, the mornings were my preference. For you, it may be during the day or at night. The beauty is, not everyone's routine will be the same. What works for you is for you. As I entered into the third leadership program, I was intentional about asking the other participants about their routine or hobbies. Not only was this informative, it was a way that I could comfortably initiate conversation – a form of networking that aligned with my goals. In the first leadership development program, I had a difficult time with this practice to the point I removed it as an intended outcome. Here, I flexed my introversion preference like I was performing an athletic event as I initiated conversations with individuals who, still, had very different lived experiences than me leading to very different routines and habits.

This leads me into another practice for self-care: Not comparing yourself to others. Theodore Roosevelt initiated the concept that "Comparison is the thief of joy[10]." You may develop a routine that works for you, but by comparing your routine to someone that has mastered their routine, you may think that your routine is less significant. Focus on yourself. Only compare yourself to your former self. Make incremental progress. Develop your routine, and know that you are not developing this routine to tell others or compare it to others. But instead, it is meant to help provide a means of self-care for yourself.

The ultimate goal is to move from having just a reserve of yourself (energy, well-being, emotional health, physical health, spiritual health, and mental health) that can be emptied (motivation) to a constant and steady stream (empowerment, strategies, routines). Finally, as we explore the constant and steady stream of empowerment, energy, and other attributes that people look to you for, I encourage you to listen to your body. This could be your body's response to certain foods, sleep patterns, exercise routines, amount of caffeine intake, or timing of all the above. Your body may respond positively or negatively to those situations. That is the thought behind listening to your body.

When you have something to give that does not empty you, the value and impact that you have is great. While there are limitless strategies for self-care, explore what has been discussed here coupled with your own knowledge, and make self-care a priority. You deserve to have rivers of physical, mental, emotional, and spiritual health to pour into others without taking from your own supply.

SUMMARY

Chapter 7 begins by drawing two analogies that illustrate the concept of self-care. Challenging the reader to look at self-care as an intentional practice, the author provides the following self-care strategies in the text:

- Recognizing the difference between productivity and busyness
- Utilizing your benefits (ex. health insurance and paid time off)
- *Developing a routine
- *Developing external hobbies
- Simplifying tasks when they become too overwhelming
- Practicing time management
- Not comparing yourself to others
- Listening to your body

The author also talks about the *power of the moment* and the *law of attraction.* When a particular moment is unsettling for you, you have the power, in that moment, to choose your reaction. This is the *power of the moment*. Based upon your choice, positive or negative energy will be attracted to you. The is the law of attraction.

> "One of the quickest and easiest ways to build resentment toward you career or company/institution is to neglect self for company."

THEORY

When individuals do not prioritize self-care, mange time well, or practice hobbies, this can lead to varying levels of stress. In the MBTI® Feedback process, Type Dynamics will be discussed which includes explaining the concept of an individual's dominant function. It would also go into explaining the auxiliary, tertiary, and inferior functions. The inferior function is the function that is the least developed and tends to be the least used. When individuals carry stress, this can lead the individual to be **In the Grip** of their inferior self. This is when their least used and least developed function – their inferior function – takes control. A symptom of being in the grip is over-exaggeration. For instance, someone with a preference for sensing tends to pay attention to detail. When in the grip, they may become obsessed with the details.

Eliminating worry is a way to help reduce stress. *Dale Carnegie* teaches the concept of **Day tight compartments.** This concept simply encourages individuals not to dwell on yesterday while not looking too far ahead into tomorrow. Rather, it encourages the focus to be on the present day. Put today into a compartment and take care of the execution of tasks for that day.

REFLECTION

When was the last time you experienced *burn out?* _____
What do you think led to this? _____
What, if anything, do you think you could have done prior to experiencing burn out? _____

APPLICATION

The author issues the challenge to develop a routine to serve as an ongoing, continuous way to facilitate self-care (asterisks in the summary). On the next page, write down 10 things – that when done – you are at your happiest or best.

Write your 10 things here.

1)	6)
2)	7)
3)	8)
4)	9)
5)	10)

Now, circle three of those ten items and commit to doing those three every day for the next three weeks. Use the tracker on the next page to keep track of your progress. After three successful weeks, add or replace one of your items if you see fit.

Week 1

SU	M	TU	W	TH	F	S
☐ ☐ ☐	☐ ☐ ☐	☐ ☐ ☐	☐ ☐ ☐	☐ ☐ ☐	☐ ☐ ☐	☐ ☐ ☐

Week 2

SU	M	TU	W	TH	F	S
☐ ☐ ☐	☐ ☐ ☐	☐ ☐ ☐	☐ ☐ ☐	☐ ☐ ☐	☐ ☐ ☐	☐ ☐ ☐

Week 3

SU	M	TU	W	TH	F	S
☐ ☐ ☐	☐ ☐ ☐	☐ ☐ ☐	☐ ☐ ☐	☐ ☐ ☐	☐ ☐ ☐	☐ ☐ ☐

8

Surrounded by Greatness

SIR ISAAC NEWTON STATED, "If I have seen further it is by standing on the shoulders of Giants"[11]. This was Newton, in an interview, acknowledging the work done by those before him that put him into a position to make significant progress. I use this quote routinely - sometimes out of context or rephrased. For instance, I may say, "I can see further by standing on the shoulders of giants." I do that to emphasize perspective, mentorship, and humility.

A common take on perspective is asking someone if they see the glass half empty or half full. Typically, if someone responds half full, their perspective is one of gratitude. On the contrary, if someone responds half empty, their perspective is typically one of lack. I like to offer a different approach. How about we, first, be grateful that we have a glass, and then two, be grateful that something is inside it - regardless of it being half full or half empty.

A part of being surrounded by greatness is being surrounded by positive energy. Rhonda Byrne, in *The Secret*, explains the Law of Attraction and how thoughts, whether positive or negative, have energy; and the energy you give off will be returned to you. A positive perspective is a positive thought. You receive, though the creative process, what you think and believe[12]. When you have a positive perspective, you are surrounding yourself with positive thoughts and positive energy. You are surrounding yourself with greatness.

Mentorship is the next concept that I extract from the shoulders of giants quote. One of the most important things that you can do in your emergence as leader is to surround yourself with individuals who can help you develop in the various areas of your life. Having someone to invest time and wisdom into you is one of the most dynamic tools that you can receive. You may think that having a mentor prior to this point was important. However, it is just as important, if not more important, to have one at this juncture of your career. Sometimes the potential mentor may be obvious and easy to establish a mentorship with. There may be other times, however, when you may have to seek out a mentor. Not only does a formal mentorship help you see further, but your friendships and peers help you see further as well. This is also defined as your circle. Is greatness found in the people you associate with, have conversations with, and live life with? Are their lifestyles consistent no matter where they are? Is it consistent no matter who they are with? And, is it consistent with your life and where you are trying to go? Do they empower you? Do they make you want to do better? If so, that is greatness! Surround yourself with these types of peers. Finally, regarding mentorship, who are you investing in? We have established the value in seeking a more seasoned mentor. We have established the need for positive, productive peers. But who are you going to be a surrounding for - meaning who are you going to mentor and invest in. Will this be someone younger? Maybe it will be someone older but has some of the same weaknesses or blind spots that you once had. The need is to be mindful as you surround yourself with greatness in the form of mentorship, to also surround someone else as they seek greatness.

Humility is the third concept I think of from this quote of seeing further. Newton did not take all of the credit. He specifically named a few individuals who, without their contributions, he would not have had the foundation to accomplish what he accomplished. A form of humility is appreciation. When I think of humility and appreciation, I continue to hear the scripture, "do not despise these small beginnings" from Zechariah 4:10. I came into my profession as an Administrative Specialist I. Through a positive perspective and great mentors, I was able to acquire more education, learn the institution, obtain higher level positions, and develop as an emerging leader. The path that I took to emerge as a leader will keep me humble with an appreciation of all levels of the institution. Humility and appreciation are two good examples of greatness. Embody these examples as you emerge as a leader.

SUMMARY

The chapter, Surrounded by Greatness, focuses on three points: perspective, mentorship, and humility. Reflecting on the **Law of Attraction**, displaying a positive perspective will surround you with positive thoughts – which is greatness. Mentorship is greatness and can be displayed as being mentored, serving as a mentor, and being a part of a circle where everyone brings value to each other – also considered as *Iron*. In Proverbs 27:17, there is an analogy of iron sharping iron as one person sharpens another person. Sharpening iron makes the material better for use. Sharpening another person is building up a person's character, confidence, overall countenance for a better life. Humility is greatness when those who paved a way are genuinely recognized as well as an appreciation for small beginnings that a leader may have had to endure in the start of their journey.

> "You may think that having a mentor prior to this point was important. However, it is just as important, if not more important, to have one at this juncture of your career."

THEORY

The three concepts of mentorships can be seen in various organizations today. In higher education, you see formal mentorship programs, peer mentoring, and student organizations all serve this purpose. In athletics you see all three levels from coach to players, player to player, and player to community. It is also prevalent in business. The mark of a true leader – and mentor – is sustainability in their programs and multiplicity of those whom they have impacted.

REFLECTION

I have had a formal mentor before. T | F

I have had an informal mentor before. T | F

I desire to have a mentor. T | F

I desire to be a mentor. T | F

I have been an informal mentor before. T | F

I have been a formal mentor before. T | F

My friends have made me better in specific areas. T | F

My friends have my best interest at heart. T | F

My friends celebrate my success. T | F

I celebrate my friends' successes. T | F

I have added value to my friends in specific areas. T | F

I have my friends' best interest at heart. T | F

APPLICATION

Focusing on quality rather than quantity, write the names of individuals who provide greatness (or has the potential to provide greatness) to you in the roles in the circle diagram below.

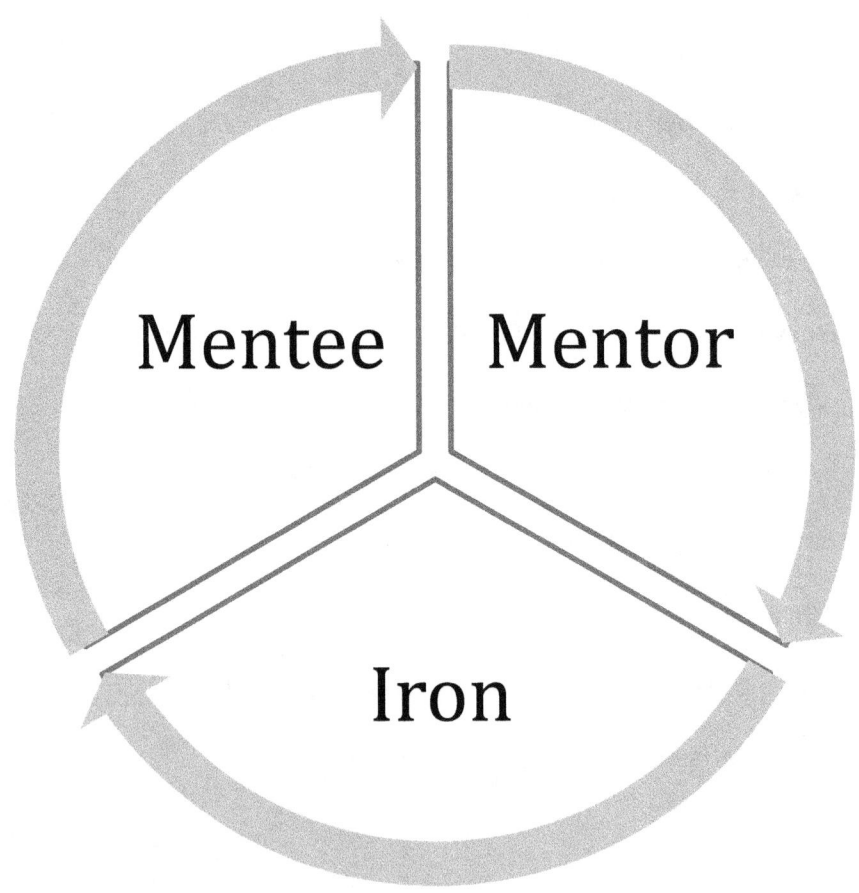

9

Still Serving

AFTER COMPLETING THE THIRD leadership program, being empowered to lead a department of 11 employees, and being responsible for six programs, the president called and asked me if I would like to serve the remainder of the term on a conference board that one of my colleagues once held. This colleague was unable to serve the remainder of her term as she was moving on to another institution out of state. I was humbled that the president would think of me, reach out to me, and ask me personally. Agreeing to serve the remainder of the term, I felt a sense of excitement and accomplishment.

This conference board that I was now serving on was through the same state organization that I went through the leadership program with. There were approximately 22 individuals in that leadership program; and including myself, four were on this conference board. The conference board had a total of approximately 23 representatives from across the state, and I was now one of these representatives! I sat in on conference calls, worked with my subcommittee, and arrived a day prior to the conference to help prepare for the next three days. I was also a presenter at this conference during one of the breakout sessions. I received my assignments, made my notes accordingly, and was in place when needed. One of the assignments was to be seated at the head table for the awards dinner. The head table, elevated on a platform, was the focal point of the room that evening. Not only was I seated there in front of all conference attendees, I was seated there in front of the attendees from my own institution - including my president and two members that were in the department that I oversaw. I was enjoying the privilege of being on the board.

Not only was being on the board an opportunity to enjoy the privileges of being distinguished, it was an opportunity to help the organization put on a good professional development opportunity for attendees to share best practices. The conference board was divided into groups that would carry out certain elements of the conference. During my initial conversations with the state organization, I was asked if I wanted to serve on a different subcommittee or remain on the subcommittee of the representative that I was replacing. Naturally since I was replacing someone, I decided to serve on the same subcommittee. I received an event badge like all the other attendees. However, my badge displayed a ribbon that distinguished me as a board member. Attendees having questions could seek out individuals with these badges. Along with answering attendee questions, behind the scenes work was carried out by the conference board. There was a group that handled the technology. They were responsible for making sure each presentation room had a projector that was working properly and that conference presenters were able to connect properly. There was a crew responsible for registration. This group would check attendees in, provide name tags, give directions, and hand out tickets that would be used for door prizes at several of the functions. There was a crew that would be available to assist the vendors, a crew to coordinate and carry out a fundraiser, and there was one last crew. This is the crew that I worked with. While I checked in with other groups to see if they needed any help, my main task would be collecting door prize tickets as conference attendees entered various sessions, breaks, and meals. While this task was not as essential as the IT crew or registration crew, my goal was to do it with excellence. I greeted the attendees as they walked in, let them know which ticket I was collecting, and I stayed at my post for the time that I was assigned. I was representing this state organization and my institution. But more importantly, I was serving the people! I was serving in a small capacity, but I was grateful to serve. I was grateful to serve not just because I was on the board. I was grateful to serve not just because I was excited about the "privilege". I was grateful to serve not just because of my ribbon on the name tag or being seated at the head table. I was grateful to serve for the sake of serving. I was grateful to serve because I felt others thought this task may have been potentially beneath them.

There are many leadership styles. When you look at the various styles, at the core, I am a servant leader. If you were to look at successful brands such as Starbucks and Aflac, you would learn that their model is one of servant leadership. I, too, believe in developing people. I believe in empowering people. I believe in listening to people. And, I believe in collaboration. I recognize that I am the leader, but I value my staff and the knowledge they bring. So, if I serve them by making sure they have the information and resources they need and continuously communicate with them and for them, I am positioning them to be successful and to adequately perform well in their roles. The more authority and status I receive, the more I find myself serving people. The more recognition I receive, the more I find myself embodying a servant's mentality. Even as I reflect on preparing to be recognized for completing the leadership program at this conference, I reflect on how my president served her husband gracefully without his prompting at this reception. This was a great reminder of humility. A reminder I received after I stepped down from the head table once the awards dinner was complete. A reminder I would receive as I took off my conference board ribbon. A reminder I would receive as we wrapped up the conference and I carried a lady's suitcase to the elevator. A reminder that I would receive as I reflected on the simplistic task of collecting door prize tickets for three days. I was reminded of the importance of steady serving. Regardless of how distinguished you are (or feel you are), you should steady serve. Regardless of how many programs you oversee, you should steady serve. Regardless of how many individuals make up your team, you should steady serve. And not only should you serve, you should do it even more as more responsibility is added to you; and you should do so gratefully and with excellence.

SUMMARY

The author attempts, in the final chapter of Experiences, to paint a picture of privilege. This picture begins with humbly accepting a position on a state conference board to sharing examples of *enjoying* the privileges that came along with it. Receiving a special designation on the name badge, being seated at the head table, and arriving a day prior to the participants, the author shared

> "I was representing this state organization and my institution. But more importantly, I was serving the people! I was serving in a small capacity, but I was grateful to serve."

these privileges with over 20 different leaders from around the state. Though the privileges were shared, the experiences were different. The author goes on to share his specific duties on the board which were less than appealing to many of the other leaders. However, with the root of the task being grounded in service, the author explains his joy in serving in that capacity.

After the privilege picture is painted, the author strips away each of the privileges presented in the artistic assembling of the analogy. The conference culminates and the author is reminded of one thing. The root of what has positioned him to this point has been service. Leaders should seek to serve gratefully and with excellence.

THEORY

- "The best way to find yourself is to lose yourself in the service of others" – Mahatma Ghandi
- "Service doesn't have to be big and grandiose to be meaningful and make a difference." – Cheryl A. Esplin

STILL SERVING

- "Leadership is service, not position." – Tim Fargo
- "Your rewards in life will be in direct proportion to the value of your service to others." – Brian Tracy
- People do not care how much you know until they know how much you care. – John C. Maxwell
- If service is below you, leadership is beyond you." – Multiple sources

REFLECTION

Do you know a leader who has embodied servant leadership?
_____

In what ways did this leader display servant leadership? _____
_____

Why do you think this leader focused on service? _____
_____

Do you consider this leader to have been an effective leader?
_____

Can you think of a leader that you know that did not display servant leadership? _____

What are some examples that make you think of this leader?
_____

Why do you think this leader did not focus on serving? _____
_____

Do you consider this leader to have been an effective leader?
_____

APPLICATION

People tend to lose the desire to serve as their roles expand and their achievements increase. Consider the roles you play. It may be leader, board member, athlete, career occupation, or otherwise. As you write down each role on the next page, imagine yourself taking off that role as if it were something you were taking off at the end of the day. When complete, you should have written down each of your roles and can visualize yourself simply as an individual. At the end of the day, we are all just individuals. When we see each other as equal, it makes it easier to serve and take interest in others.

STILL SERVING

1. _____
2. _____
3. _____
4. _____
5. _____
6. _____
7. _____
8. _____
9. _____
10. _____
11. _____
12. _____
13. _____
14. _____
15. _____

10

The Planner

I HOPE THAT YOU HAVE SEEN the importance of leading self and that leadership competencies can be learned and developed. Throughout my emerging leadership journey, I have had to do three things before I could fully execute in this role. I had to know the role, understand the role, and accept the role. These key principles would provide me with the perspective I needed when planning, communicating, facilitating, and following up. When one knows, understands, and accepts their role, they can better understand how their role (and their value) fits into the overall process. The next step is to have a system in order to properly execute.

The Planner is meant to help you with a system to better lead yourself. This planner is intended to initiate internal work to facilitate best practices for leading self as we have learned that we must first lead ourselves before we can effectively lead others.

VISION

Theme: [Develop a theme (or a focus) for a specific period of time. You may decide on one month, three months, one semester, or the

THE PLANNER

full year. This practice is to help you chart a course of action. This practice directly relates to the leadership competency of vision.]

MINDSET

Goals: [Personal themes can tend to have a cliché effect to them. This is why the competency of mindset is of importance. You have read the chapter *Where is the Power* and learned about the ownership mentality. A practical way to own your theme is to set weekly or monthly goals based on this theme.]

Tasks: [Similar to goals and themes, your tasks will correlate with your goals. Tasks should be more practical things you plan to do rather than what you are trying to accomplish (goal).]

RELATIONSHIPS

Resources Needed: [In the relationship competency, being the right person, mentorship, and servanthood are essential elements. Not all of the resources you will need in order to accomplish your tasks and goals will be tangible. Some of these resources may be in the form of people. Some of the resources you may need may be provided to you by people. Some of the resources you currently have, someone else may be able to benefit from. This section is to self-assess what you need in order to meet your goals – in addition to assessing what you have that others may need to reach their goals.]

Example: Monthly Theme, Weekly Goals, Daily Tasks **This is Week 1**	
Theme:	**EXECUTION**
Goal 1:	**Be more strategic with my time**
Task:	Awake/Begin morning routine 30 minutes earlier than normal 3 out of 5 workdays
Task:	Listen to some form of personal development during lunch
Goal 2:	**Improve in 2 *areas of reflection* as identified in chapter 6 of the *Workbook for Emerging Leaders***
Task:	Listen to an informative speech on the internet regarding the topic(s) at least one per day
Task:	Identify a book in the local/college library or on Amazon about the topic that you will consider looking into further next week
Task:	Identify a reputable expert in this area to consider learning more about

THE PLANNER

VISION

Theme: [___EXECUTION_____]

MINDSET

Goals: [_(1) Be more strategic with my time_____]
[_(2) Improve in 2 areas of reflection from WB Chp 6_____]
[_____]

Tasks: [_(1) Awake / Begin morning routine 30 mins earlier than normal 3 out of workdays_____]
[_(1) Listen to some form of personal development during lunch_]
[_____]
[_(2) Identify a book on the topic that I will read_____]
[_(2) Identify a reputable expert to learn more about_____]

RELATIONSHIPS

Resources Needed: [_____]
[_Library access_____]
[_Youtube_____]
[_TedTalks or some form of podcast - Do I know someone that can recommend a person or platform_____]
[_____]

Notes for Self - Home
You can write notes that are specific to your personal life here such as home, children, spouse, etc. Then, you can organize them into your week in the bottom right quadrant.

Notes for Self - Professionally
You can write notes that are specific to your profession here. Then, you can organize them into your week in the bottom right quadrant.

Notes for Self - Random
You can write notes that are not specific for home or your profession here. Then, you can organize them into your week using the quadrant to the right.

Tasks for Sunday
Set tasks for the week here.

Tasks for Monday
Include just a few major tasks as not to overwhelm yourself.

Tasks for Tuesday
~~Mark through tasks as you complete them.~~

Tasks for Wednesday

Tasks for Thursday

Tasks for Friday

Tasks for Saturday

THE PLANNER

VISION
Theme: [_____]

MINDSET
Goals: [_____]
[_____]
[_____]

Tasks: [_____]
[_____]
[_____]
[_____]
[_____]

RELATIONSHIPS
Resources Needed: [_____]
[_____]
[_____]
[_____]
[_____]

LEADERSHIP EXPERIENCES

Notes for Self – [   ]

Notes for Self – [   ]

Notes for Self – [   ]

Tasks for Sunday

Tasks for Monday

Tasks for Tuesday

Tasks for Wednesday

Tasks for Thursday

Tasks for Friday

Tasks for Saturday

THE PLANNER

VISION
Theme: [_____]

MINDSET
Goals: [_____]
[_____]
[_____]

Tasks: [_____]
[_____]
[_____]
[_____]
[_____]

RELATIONSHIPS
Resources Needed: [_____]
[_____]
[_____]
[_____]
[_____]

LEADERSHIP EXPERIENCES

Notes for Self – [   ]

Notes for Self – [   ]

Notes for Self – [   ]

Tasks for Sunday

Tasks for Monday

Tasks for Tuesday

Tasks for Wednesday

Tasks for Thursday

Tasks for Friday

Tasks for Saturday

THE PLANNER

VISION
Theme: [_____]

MINDSET
Goals: [_____]
[_____]
[_____]

Tasks: [_____]
[_____]
[_____]
[_____]
[_____]

RELATIONSHIPS
Resources Needed: [_____]
[_____]
[_____]
[_____]
[_____]

LEADERSHIP EXPERIENCES

Notes for Self – [   ]

Notes for Self – [   ]

Notes for Self – [   ]

Tasks for Sunday

Tasks for Monday

Tasks for Tuesday

Tasks for Wednesday

Tasks for Thursday

Tasks for Friday

Tasks for Saturday

THE PLANNER

VISION
Theme: [_____]

MINDSET
Goals: [_____]
[_____]
[_____]

Tasks: [_____]
[_____]
[_____]
[_____]
[_____]

RELATIONSHIPS
Resources Needed: [_____]
[_____]
[_____]
[_____]
[_____]

LEADERSHIP EXPERIENCES

Notes for Self – [ ]	Notes for Self – [ ]

Notes for Self – [ ]	
	Tasks for Sunday
	Tasks for Monday
	Tasks for Tuesday
	Tasks for Wednesday
	Tasks for Thursday
	Tasks for Friday
	Tasks for Saturday

THE PLANNER

VISION
Theme: [_____]

MINDSET
Goals: [_____]
[_____]
[_____]

Tasks: [_____]
[_____]
[_____]
[_____]
[_____]

RELATIONSHIPS
Resources Needed: [_____]
[_____]
[_____]
[_____]
[_____]

LEADERSHIP EXPERIENCES

Notes for Self – [ ]	Notes for Self – [ ]

Notes for Self – [ ]	
	Tasks for Sunday
	Tasks for Monday
	Tasks for Tuesday
	Tasks for Wednesday
	Tasks for Thursday
	Tasks for Friday
	Tasks for Saturday

THE PLANNER

VISION
Theme: [_____]

MINDSET
Goals: [_____]
[_____]
[_____]

Tasks: [_____]
[_____]
[_____]
[_____]
[_____]

RELATIONSHIPS
Resources Needed: [_____]
[_____]
[_____]
[_____]
[_____]

LEADERSHIP EXPERIENCES

Notes for Self – [   ]

Notes for Self – [   ]

Notes for Self – [   ]

Tasks for Sunday

Tasks for Monday

Tasks for Tuesday

Tasks for Wednesday

Tasks for Thursday

Tasks for Friday

Tasks for Saturday

THE PLANNER

VISION
Theme: [_____]

MINDSET
Goals: [_____]
[_____]
[_____]

Tasks: [_____]
[_____]
[_____]
[_____]
[_____]

RELATIONSHIPS
Resources Needed: [_____]
[_____]
[_____]
[_____]
[_____]

LEADERSHIP EXPERIENCES

Notes for Self – [   ]

Notes for Self – [   ]

Notes for Self – [   ]

Tasks for Sunday

Tasks for Monday

Tasks for Tuesday

Tasks for Wednesday

Tasks for Thursday

Tasks for Friday

Tasks for Saturday

THE PLANNER

VISION
Theme: [_____]

MINDSET
Goals: [_____]

[_____]

[_____]

Tasks: [_____]

[_____]

[_____]

[_____]

[_____]

RELATIONSHIPS
Resources Needed: [_____]

[_____]

[_____]

[_____]

[_____]

LEADERSHIP EXPERIENCES

Notes for Self – [   ]

Notes for Self – [   ]

Notes for Self – [   ]

Tasks for Sunday

Tasks for Monday

Tasks for Tuesday

Tasks for Wednesday

Tasks for Thursday

Tasks for Friday

Tasks for Saturday

THE PLANNER

VISION
Theme: [_____]

MINDSET
Goals: [_____]
[_____]
[_____]

Tasks: [_____]
[_____]
[_____]
[_____]
[_____]

RELATIONSHIPS
Resources Needed: [_____]
[_____]
[_____]
[_____]
[_____]

LEADERSHIP EXPERIENCES

| Notes for Self – [   ] | Notes for Self – [   ] |

Notes for Self – [   ]

Tasks for Sunday

Tasks for Monday

Tasks for Tuesday

Tasks for Wednesday

Tasks for Thursday

Tasks for Friday

Tasks for Saturday

THE PLANNER

VISION
Theme: [_____]

MINDSET
Goals: [_____]
[_____]
[_____]

Tasks: [_____]
[_____]
[_____]
[_____]
[_____]

RELATIONSHIPS
Resources Needed: [_____]
[_____]
[_____]
[_____]
[_____]

LEADERSHIP EXPERIENCES

Notes for Self – [   ]

Notes for Self – [   ]

Notes for Self – [   ]

Tasks for Sunday

Tasks for Monday

Tasks for Tuesday

Tasks for Wednesday

Tasks for Thursday

Tasks for Friday

Tasks for Saturday

THE PLANNER

VISION
Theme: [_____]

MINDSET
Goals: [_____]
[_____]
[_____]

Tasks: [_____]
[_____]
[_____]
[_____]
[_____]

RELATIONSHIPS
Resources Needed: [_____]
[_____]
[_____]
[_____]
[_____]

LEADERSHIP EXPERIENCES

Notes for Self – [ ]	Notes for Self – [ ]

Notes for Self – [ ]	
	Tasks for Sunday
	Tasks for Monday
	Tasks for Tuesday
	Tasks for Wednesday
	Tasks for Thursday
	Tasks for Friday
	Tasks for Saturday

THE PLANNER

VISION
Theme: [_____]

MINDSET
Goals: [_____]
[_____]
[_____]

Tasks: [_____]
[_____]
[_____]
[_____]
[_____]

RELATIONSHIPS
Resources Needed: [_____]
[_____]
[_____]
[_____]
[_____]

LEADERSHIP EXPERIENCES

Notes for Self – [   ]

Notes for Self – [   ]

Notes for Self – [   ]

Tasks for Sunday

Tasks for Monday

Tasks for Tuesday

Tasks for Wednesday

Tasks for Thursday

Tasks for Friday

Tasks for Saturday

THE PLANNER

VISION
Theme: [_____]

MINDSET
Goals: [_____]
[_____]
[_____]

Tasks: [_____]
[_____]
[_____]
[_____]
[_____]

RELATIONSHIPS
Resources Needed: [_____]
[_____]
[_____]
[_____]
[_____]

LEADERSHIP EXPERIENCES

| Notes for Self – [   ] | Notes for Self – [   ] |

| Notes for Self – [   ] |

Tasks for Sunday

Tasks for Monday

Tasks for Tuesday

Tasks for Wednesday

Tasks for Thursday

Tasks for Friday

Tasks for Saturday

THE PLANNER

VISION
Theme: [_____]

MINDSET
Goals: [_____]
[_____]
[_____]

Tasks: [_____]
[_____]
[_____]
[_____]
[_____]

RELATIONSHIPS
Resources Needed: [_____]
[_____]
[_____]
[_____]
[_____]

LEADERSHIP EXPERIENCES

Notes for Self – [   ]

Notes for Self – [   ]

Notes for Self – [   ]

Tasks for Sunday

Tasks for Monday

Tasks for Tuesday

Tasks for Wednesday

Tasks for Thursday

Tasks for Friday

Tasks for Saturday

THE PLANNER

VISION
Theme: [_____]

MINDSET
Goals: [_____]
[_____]
[_____]

Tasks: [_____]
[_____]
[_____]
[_____]
[_____]

RELATIONSHIPS
Resources Needed: [_____]
[_____]
[_____]
[_____]
[_____]

LEADERSHIP EXPERIENCES

Notes for Self – [　　　　　]

Notes for Self – [　　　　　]

Notes for Self – [　　　　　]

Tasks for Sunday

Tasks for Monday

Tasks for Tuesday

Tasks for Wednesday

Tasks for Thursday

Tasks for Friday

Tasks for Saturday

THE PLANNER

VISION
Theme: [_____]

MINDSET
Goals: [_____]
[_____]
[_____]

Tasks: [_____]
[_____]
[_____]
[_____]
[_____]

RELATIONSHIPS
Resources Needed: [_____]
[_____]
[_____]
[_____]
[_____]

LEADERSHIP EXPERIENCES

Notes for Self – [   ]

Notes for Self – [   ]

Notes for Self – [   ]

Tasks for Sunday

Tasks for Monday

Tasks for Tuesday

Tasks for Wednesday

Tasks for Thursday

Tasks for Friday

Tasks for Saturday

REFERENCES

Byrne, R. (2006). The secret. New York: Hillsboro, Ore: Atria Books
Cauthron, Anne (2016). Managers vs. Leaders. Union County Leadership Academy.

Covey, S. R. (2004). *The 7 habits of highly effective people: Restoring the character ethic* ([Rev. ed.].). New York: Free Press.

DR Services, Principles of Management. The Five Stages of Team Development.
https://courses.lumenlearning.com/suny-principlesmanagement/chapter/reading-the-five-stages-of-team-development/

Dungy, T. (2012). Uncommon Manhood: Secrets to What It Means to Be a Man. Tyndale House Publisher, Inc.

Evans, N.J., Forney, D.S., Guido, F.M., Patton, L.D., Reen, K.A. (2010). Student Development in College: Theory Research, and Practice. 2nd Edition; Jossey-Bass

Graduation Wisdom: Randy Pausch. (2009, June 26). Retrieved December 19, 2019, from https://www.graduationwisdom.com/speeches/0039-pausch.htm.

Maxwell, J.C.(2007). The 21 Irrefutable Laws of Leadership. 10th anniversary edition. Thomas Nelson.Stanley, A. (2011, August 17). Leaders who refuse to listen will eventually be surrounded by people who have nothing significant to say. Retrieved December 19, 2019, from
https://twitter.com/andystanley/status/103841035108630528?lang=en.

Maxwell, J. C. (2011). *The five levels of leadership: Proven steps to maximize your potential*.

Ortega, S. (2015, November 9). Inflight passenger announcements. Retrieved December 19, 2019, from https://airodyssey.net/reference/inflight/#safety.

Segovia, M. (2019, December). Type Dynamics. MBTI Certification Program.

Stream. (n.d.). Retrieved December 19, 2019, from https://www.merriam-webster.com/dictionary/stream.

Theodore Roosevelt Quotes (Author of The Rough Riders) (page 2 of 14). (n.d.). Retrieved December 19, 2019, from
https://www.goodreads.com/author/quotes/44567.Theodore_Roosevelt?page=2.

Thomas, E (2018, August 5). *WHAT'S YOUR WHY (Eric Thomas Motivation)*. Retrieved from https://www.youtube.com/watch?v=euH2DpY7BQI

Vernon, J. L. (n.d.) *Shoulders of giants.* Retreived December 19, 2019 from https://www.americanscientist.org/article/on-the-shoulders-of-giants.

LEADERSHIP EXPERIENCES
The Series for Emerging Leaders

www.ingramcontent.com/pod-product-compliance
Lightning Source LLC
Chambersburg PA
CBHW070832300426
44111CB00014B/2534